"God has a way of empowering Kent, as movement, to speak to the heart of very style that moves along with ease and encourages the reader on nearly every page. His own "business as ministry" life experiences shape much of this work and offer the reader deep insight as well as personal enrichment."

Dr. Mark Cress
Founder / President
Corporate Chaplains of America, Inc.

"In Opening Doors, Kent clearly explains how to be a natural, relevant ambassador for Jesus Christ in the workplace. The simple Biblical truths in this book are reinforced with powerful stories and practical examples. Kent's passion to see this message spread comes across vividly in this wonderful resource."

Eric Welch
National Facilitator of Ministry Network
Mission America Coalition

"Kent's contagious passion for others with the hope of Christ bubbles out on every page. As a fully devoted Jesus follower, he is able to lead the reader to understanding the keys to engagement that count. Unlocking doors in the workplace is truly an "inside job" and Kent's message will help pick locks with Heavenly expertise."

Richard S. DeWitt
President & COO
Marketplace Chaplains USA

"Kent Humphreys clearly explains the Kingdom of God through the business perspective. Kent prepares us for the work of service in our everyday life interactions. This is a must read for those of us with callings in the marketplace."

Al Caperna
CEO, CMC Group
Director, call2all Business Track

Kent Humphreys is an example to me of a man who has faithfully allowed Jesus to live through him in his roles of CEO, leader, and owner for many, many years. The true test of one's values is provided by time as both the good and the hard seasons come along. Kent shows us how God opens the door for any who desire to live consistent lives of significance and spiritual fruitfulness.

Buck Jacobs
Chairman and Founder
The C12 Group, LLC

For years Kent Humphreys has poured out his life to advance God's Kingdom through business. In Opening Doors, he shares Biblical examples and personal stories to reveal how simple it really is to be a fruitful follower of Christ in the marketplace. If that's your desire, put these practical insights to work and enjoy the adventure with God!

Chris Duncan
CEO
Convene

Ephesians 4:11-13 refers to individuals God has given to the church to prepare God's people for works of service. Kent Humphreys is one of those given to the Christian community. The church is not real estate, nor is it an event...it is people. This book helps business people discover and thrive in their calling and ministry.

Paul Richardson
President CBMC

KENT HUMPHREYS

CHRIST@WORK
OPENING
DOORS

Impacting your Workplace for Jesus Christ

Published by
Lifestyle Impact Ministries
Kent Humphreys
PO Box 271054
Oklahoma City, OK 73137-1054
Phone: 405-949-0070 x102 or 405-917-1681 x102
Email: kent@fcci.org or khumphreys@ahpartners.com
Website: www.lifestyleimpact.com

Book design: C R Design, Charles Rogez, 405-550-9176

Some of the anecdotal illustrations in this book are true to life and are included with the
permission of the persons involved. All other illustrations are composites of real situa-
tions, and any resemblance to people living or dead is coincidental.

Unless otherwise identified, all Scripture quotations in this publication are taken from
the HOLY BIBLE: NEW AMERICAN STANDARD VERSION® (nasv®). Copyright
© 1973, 1978, 1984 by International Bible Society. Used by permission of Zondervan
Publishing House. All rights reserved. Other versions used include: the New International
Version (NIV), © The Lockman Foundation 1960, 1962, 1963, 1968, 1971, 1972, 1973,
1975, 1977; The New Testament in Modern English (ph), J. B. Phillips Translator, © J. B.
Phillips 1958, 1960, 1972, used by permission of Macmillan Publishing Company; THE
MESSAGE (msg). Copyright © 1993, 1994, 1995, 1996, 2000, 2001, 2002. Used by
permission of NavPress Publishing Group; The Living Bible (tlb), Copyright © 1971, used
by permission of Tyndale House Publishers, Inc., Wheaton, IL 60189, all rights reserved;
and the Good News Bible Today's English ersion (tev), copyright © American Bible
Society 1966, 1971, 1976.

Humphreys, Kent.
  Christ @ Work - Opening Doors. Impacting your Workplace for Jesus Christ
Includes bibliographical references.
  1. Evangelistic work. 2. Witness bearing (Christianity) 3.Work--Religious aspects--
Christianity. I. Title.

ISBN: 978-0-9843575-0-5

9 780984 357505

IN MEMORY OF

Bruce E. Alleman

*whose life exemplified
the principles
presented in the book*

CONTENTS

Note: Unless otherwise noted, all Scriptures are quoted from the New American Standard Version (NASV).

FORWARD

Have you ever felt like a square peg trying to fit into a round hole? I have felt exactly that way along my life's journey. After enjoying a career in the US Nuclear Navy Submarine Force, I entered a successful business in San Diego, California. I attended a great church and my life should have felt fulfilled, but it wasn't; something was missing.

When I met Kent Humphreys, we immediately "clicked" as friends. We soon discovered that we had gone through a similar square peg experience. People like Kent and myself feel lost or, more aptly, incomplete inside the church walls --- we want to be equipped by our church to find kingdom significance and purpose where we interact with culture, outside the church walls. We long to see God work through our work! From research and experience, I've come to understand that there are millions of us who feel disconnected from our true purpose at work.

Maybe you've had feelings at times that are similar. You sense your job or career has something critically important to do with God's bigger story, and yet no one seems to be there to help you understand how it really works and why it is so biblical. Maybe, like me, something inside you believes your work really is ministry. The actual work itself is an act of ministry!

Let me stop right now and say you must read this book! Reading it will change your perspective! Kent deals with this subject head on in way that is both refreshing and real. He has put together a practical guide to help all of us focus on five key questions from Scripture that will revolutionize our joy and effectiveness at work – no matter the vocation in which you or I find ourselves. The real life stories in this book make it a true adventure that will captivate you instead of making you feel it's just another "to-do" list. Read it. Live it!

As one of the most authentic workplace believers I know, Kent's lifelong journey through the trials and successes of work make him a seasoned practitioner and teacher. His book is filled with both biblical truths and practical tools. Keep the five key questions on your radar as you work - they will function as a GPS system keeping you on track for real spiritual success at work. You will see Christ's intentions for your life at work – you can see His Open Doors!

I appreciate Kent for tackling this critical issue. May God bless you as you read and apply these graceful life changing truths.

Doug Spada
Founder and CEO
of WorkLife.org

ACKNOWLEDGEMENTS

My wife, Davidene, has been my constant encourager, advisor, editor, and partner in this project. Without her sacrificial work, writing skills, and sage wisdom, this work would have never been completed. This is the fifth book that we have done together. She has encouraged me to finally write on my passion, impacting the workplace for Christ. I have spoken on this subject for twenty years, but I have never been able to put these simple truths into written words. God has gifted her with the ability to help me to do that and to help many others pursue their literary dreams.

I am grateful for the tireless work of my assistant, Kristen Jones, whose creative and administrative genius makes me far more effective than I ever thought possible. She is a constant joy to work with and gives great energy to every project.

Thank you, Chad Rogez, for being the best graphic and layout artist that we have ever worked with. He is truly amazing in bringing our dreams into focus and visual representation. The editorial assistance of Linda Sageser has been invaluable in all the details.

This work would have not been possible without the continual encouragement of Doug Hunter and the staff and volunteer leadership of Fellowship of Companies for Christ, International. They have supported me in my role as a worldwide ambassador for FCCI and kept after me to put these thoughts into writing. FCCI has graciously allowed me to use their Christ@Work brand for the book and the entire workplace series that we will be doing under that brand.

I have been greatly impacted by the many other leaders in the worldwide workplace movement, and am indebted to men like Doug Spada, Os Hillman, Patrick O'Neal, Buck Jacobs, Al Caperna and so many others who are kingdom partners in this global move of God.

Finally, without the mentoring and example of my father, Jack Humphreys, along with Gene Warr, Ford Madison, Pete Hammond, and others I would have never been able to channel the passion that I have for reaching the workplace. I humbly acknowledge that I am just a businessman who has been touched by Christ and impacted by hundreds of other fellow workplace believers in the daily challenges of the marketplace.

Kent Humphreys

INTRODUCTION

"So <u>naturally</u> we proclaim Christ! We warn every man we meet and teach everyone we can, all that we know about Him, so that if possible we may bring every man up to his full maturity in Christ Jesus. This is what I am working at all the time with all the strength that God gives me."

Colossians 1:28, 29 (Phillips)

I want to share with you <u>five</u> simple truths that will eternally change how you view yourself and your workplace. We will do this by answering five questions. I have shared these principles with followers of Jesus across the United States and around the globe over the last twenty years, and they are universal. They work in my hometown of Oklahoma City and in Portland, Oregon. They have been proven in Albuquerque, New Mexico, and Raleigh, North Carolina. My fellow followers of Christ in the workplace have put these into practice in Kuala Lumpur, Malaysia, and in Amsterdam. They have been implemented in Cape Town, South Africa, and in Mexico City. I will base these on biblical examples throughout the scriptures and use real life stories out of my workplace experience over the last forty years. I will show you practical tools that you can adapt to your personality, gifting, and workplace. Although I have primarily been in the business arena as a business owner, specifically in the distribution and real estate areas, these principles will work for you in whatever sphere that God has sovereignly placed you and in whatever your position that you find yourself. You may work in a government position or in education, in the media or in entertainment. You may be in a church, in a religious ministry, or in the marketplace in areas such as manufacturing, or retail, or transportation. After understanding these five principles, you will view your work differently than ever before. You will go each day to your workplace with a new sense of calling and affirmation.

I have found that about 80 percent of people in our churches do not understand these teachings from the Scriptures. These church members have been blinded by the idea that our spiritual life or church involvement is to be totally separate from our work life. Not only has the secular culture pushed this idea, but our own religious organizations have led to this wrong thinking by our teaching and the modeling of our "full-time" religious leaders. This "dualistic" thinking of separating our lives into the *secular* and the *spiritual* has hampered the Body of Christ from being all that God wants us to be in our sphere of influence in our everyday lives. My friend, Walt Henrichsen, says that the "spiritual" or "religious" activities that we do become "secular" if done for the temporal. However, the "secular" becomes "spiritual" if done for the eternal. So, the key is our objective and viewpoint. In the following chapters we will consider the principles that will help you turn your secular workplace into a spiritual investment.

My personal journey into a realization that God intended for my relationship with Him to be lived out in the marketplace happened like this. In the 1960's, I carefully watched Christian business leaders who were my mentors in the marketplace, and I began to learn how to walk with God. In the 70's, I learned how to integrate my faith and my work. Then, in the 80's, my brothers and I began to experiment on how to use our distribution business as a platform for ministry to our co-workers. In the 90's, while still running our company, I traveled on weekends to share these truths with other CEO's, business owners, and workplace leaders across the United States. Finally, for the last ten years I have been able to travel around the globe meeting with leaders in many nations discussing these biblical truths which are applicable to every marketplace. My hope for you is that you will understand these truths from the Word of God and apply them to your life throughout your week.

May the Holy Spirit allow you to manifest Jesus to those around you in such a way that their lives are impacted for Christ. This will not only result in evangelism of those who do not know Christ, as well as discipling and mentoring of those who do know Him, but you will be an example to those around you of one who enjoys their profession and does it with excellence. You will provide financially for your family and be a positive influence to all with whom you come in contact. You will walk through the "open doors" that Christ provides in your sphere of influence, and by doing so, you will forever impact your co-workers, customers, vendors, and even your competitors. Christ's work in your own life will produce transformation that will be visible to everyone, and the Lord uses such a life as a magnet to draw people to Himself.

So, before we get started with the first question, look at the verses above from Colossians 1. This passage will be the foundation for all that we say. Read these verses slowly a couple of times. Let the words sink into your mind. Notice that we are to "*proclaim Christ*". This is not an option. We are to do this "*naturally*". This is not a system or a process but an overflow of our daily lives. We proclaim a person, not a religious organization. "*Warning*" people is evangelism, and "*teaching*" is discipling them. We simply pass on to others what Jesus has been showing to us as we walk with Him. The reason that many of us are not passing things on is that we do not have a daily vital relationship with the risen Christ. We cannot share with others if we do not "know Him" in a personal way.

The goal is to bring the people around us up to "*their full maturity in Christ*". This means not only our family members and our friends at church or in our Bible study, but our co-workers as well. That is where we spend the bulk of our hours during the week. God has placed us into that workplace for a specific purpose. Paul explains that this task is not to be done just on Sunday or a few times a week, but this is a 24/7 "*all-the-time*" assignment from God. And the final words may be the most important of all. When I share these thoughts with aggressive workplace leaders, they want to charge off and do something for Jesus. However, the lasting spiritual fruit will come when we find that the Holy Spirit alone gives us the power to manifest the risen Christ. We need to keep our focus on Him and allow *God to give us His strength* to complete this impossible task.

So, re-read these verses from Colossians, chapter one, a few more times. You may want to memorize and meditate on them and ask God to show you how they relate to your daily life in your workplace. Consider again the meaning of naturally evangelizing, discipling, modeling, knowing Christ, gaining full maturity, doing it 24/7, and appropriating the power of the Holy Spirit within us. Then get ready for our journey. We will start with the first question in chapter one. To do that, I want to share with you a shocking story concerning a curse!

An Example from the life of Daniel:

I want to introduce you to my favorite Bible character, Daniel. We will use his life as a biblical example for each of the five truths that we will be presenting. The book of Daniel has 12 chapters; the first six cover his life story, and the last six chapters deal with prophecy. My question for you is this. How old was Daniel when he was thrown into the lion's den? You may have studied his life when you were a young child in your church and have an impression in your mind about his age. Write it down, and we will share the answer in a later chapter.

CHAPTER ONE
Who is to do it?

OUR CALLING IS TO REPRESENT JESUS CHRIST TO OTHERS

"That God was reconciling the world to himself in Christ, not counting men's sins against them. And he has committed to us the message of reconciliation. We are therefore Christ's ambassadors, as though God were making his appeal through us. We implore you on Christ's behalf: be reconciled to God."

2 Corinthians 5:19-20

Simon walked into his kitchen and found the largest knife there. He placed the knife inside his jacket pocket and left to go to his office. He was planning to murder his boss because he had been stuck at home on probation. When Simon arrived at the office, he was met by two men, the receptionist and the accountant. One of the men began to quote John 3: 16, "For God so loved the world that he gave his one and only Son, that whoever believes in him shall not perish but have eternal life." This prompted a discussion which ended four hours later at the accountant's home. Simon fell to his knees that afternoon and asked Jesus Christ to come into his life. He called his wife and told her that while he was on the way to murder his boss, he met Jesus Christ.

These events happened in 1990, and over the next six years Simon was employed in the workplace. Then in 1996, Simon felt the call of God on his life to become a pastor, so he quit his job and started attending a small seminary. He leased out his van to a taxi driver for extra income. This plan failed when he was defrauded out of the vehicle. Simon soon began to pastor a small church in the slums while going to school. For the next four years, Simon went to school and pastored the small church, and his wife provided some income. Finally, in a financial crisis in 2000, Simon's wife appealed to him to give up the schooling and pastorate and get a job to provide for the family, because they were eleven months behind on their rent. She reminded Simon of his Biblical responsibility to provide for the family. After considering her words, Simon went to the country to see his father and explain to him that he was giving up the pastorate, at least for a time.

When Simon arrived at his father's home and explained the situation, his father asked him to sit down while he went to fetch Simon's brother and mother. His father shared with them a story that Simon had never heard. The father explained that in 1966, a few days after Simon's birth, he stood up in front of his church one morning and resigned his position as pastor. When he was finished, the associate pastor stood and pronounced a curse on Simon's father. When the bishop was in town a few days later, Simon's father appealed the matter to the bishop. Finally, the three men agreed that the baby, Simon, would one day become a pastor. As long as Simon remained a pastor, the "curse" would not affect Simon's father or pass on to Simon or to Simon's children. So, Simon's father explained that there was no way that Simon could give up the pastorate. The safety of the family was depending on him remaining in the pastoral ministry. (Note: This took place in Kenya, Africa, where family curses are a common occurrence because of centuries-old false religious beliefs). Simon left his father's home and returned to his wife, not knowing what to do.

That summer, Simon was to go to Amsterdam, Holland, to meet with 10,000 other evangelists from all over the world at "Amsterdam 2000", an event sponsored by the Billy Graham organization. The cost for each participant was about $2,000 of which Simon was to pay $150. He showed up at the plane and told the conference planners that he did not have the money. They allowed him to get on the plane anyway, and Simon was off to Amsterdam. When he arrived there, he found himself with 7,000 other leaders from all over the world, in a dorm setting, in large buildings on the outskirts of Amsterdam. That Tuesday, Simon woke up in the middle of the night and prayed that God would lead him to the one person who could help him with his dilemma. When he awoke on Wednesday morning at 6 a.m., he again prayed for God to give him someone to help him with an answer to his problem.

That morning Simon showed up at the counseling center where I was meeting one-on-one with participants. Simon was assigned to me and sat across the table while he shared his story. I asked Simon if he believed in the sovereignty of God. I shared with him that there were 90 counselors out of the 10,000 participants who were meeting with them to help on personal and ministry issues. Of the 90 counselors, 45 were used in small group video sessions. Of the remaining 45, 31 were professionally trained Christian counselors from around the world. Eight of them were pastors, including my own pastor and my son who is a pastor. The final six were from the marketplace. Of the six, I was the only one that had dealt with the issue that Simon had encountered. I, also, had left the workplace to prepare for pastoral ministry, and had also been led back into business. In fact, I had spoken about this issue to business leaders and to pastors across our nation. So, I explained to Simon that God had answered his prayer and led him to the one person who knew something about what he was going through, and could answer his question. Then I silently prayed for God's help as I had no idea what to say next!

I first told Simon that by the authority of Scripture I could assure him that he was not under the curse. Galatians 3:13 says, "*Christ redeemed us from the curse of the law by becoming a curse for us, for it is written: "Cursed is everyone who is hung on a tree."* Jesus not only took our sins on the cross but actually became a curse for us. Therefore, no follower of Jesus ever has to endure a curse of any kind.

I then asked Simon to turn with me to Hebrews, chapter 11. If you have your Bible handy, why not turn with me to that passage right now? I told Simon that I would read the names of these men and women in the "Hall of Faith" and would have him tell me whether they were religious professionals or just ordinary people in the workplace. So, we found that:

Abel was a herdsman

Noah was in the construction business

Abraham, Isaac, and Jacob were shepherds

Sarah was a mother

Joseph was a government official

Moses was a political leader

Rahab was a prostitute

Gideon was a military leader

Samson was a judge

David was a king

Finally, we got to Samuel, who was a prophet. Samuel and maybe one other person out of the entire list were professional religious leaders. All the other men and women were out in the workplace doing many different things. So, I was able to explain to Simon, that by the authority of God's Word, I could assure him that he would not be under the curse if he left the pastorate. I did not know for sure what God's specific will for him was, but I knew that he was free to be in education or business or another profession, with God's blessing. A big smile came on Simon's face. He returned to Kenya, found another job, and started a business. Today he is a pastor of a church and has a ministry in Kenya which I hope to visit in the future.

You may say to yourselves, "How foolish to think that he could be under a curse for leaving the vocational ministry!" However, in your own church most of the people that you sat next to last Sunday morning have figurative shackles on their ankles, handcuffs on their wrists, and blinders on their eyes because they believe that they are "second class citizens" in terms of ministry. They believe that the pastor, the missionary, the church staff, and the para-church organization workers are chosen, gifted, and paid to do the professional ministry. They think that their job is to fund the work of God through their giving and to help support the professionals to lead the effort. They do not realize that they will come into contact with and influence more people in one day in the workplace than the professionals will encounter in a week or even a full month. They have no concept that they are ambassadors for God in the marketplace.

Yes, YOU are in full-time ministry for Jesus Christ, but you get your income from your employment in the workplace and not from your church. What a bargain for God's kingdom work. We are paid by the secular world's system yet are placed there in strategic positions for His purposes. We are all called by God as his specific representatives in our sphere of influence. He has a special plan for each of our lives everyday. 2 Timothy 1:9 NASU tells us that this is a holy calling, "who has saved us and called us with a holy calling, not according to our works, but according to His own purpose and grace which was granted us in Christ Jesus from all eternity." Five verses later in verse 14, Paul reminds us, "Guard, through the Holy Spirit who dwells in us, the treasure which has been entrusted to you." Each of us has been given unique personalities, talents, gifts, backgrounds, and circumstances which are to be used for the glory of Christ. While we need to understand our uniqueness, the key to our usefulness will be our availability to be used by Him in any circumstance. We are full-time ambassadors for the King of Kings on call 24 hours a day.

In my own life I felt the sincere "call" of God on my life when I was seventeen years of age. At that time I believed that if you really loved Jesus, you had to be a missionary or a pastor. I did not think that I could make it as a missionary, so I thought that God must have called me to the pastoral ministry. My plan was to enter a secular university in my home state and afterward go to seminary. I was encouraged to take ten hours of Greek my freshman year. I also took science, English, and history, while ignoring my favorite subjects of math and business. I was "suffering for Jesus" by following the calling of God on my life. By my sophomore year I was nearly flunking out of school. I met a young man who worked with students at another campus. He spent a Saturday morning with me. He shared with me that I could go into business where I had talents and experience, and still be used by Christ. The next day I switched my major to business, and my grades rose dramatically. It was easy for me, and I enjoyed nearly every class.

That was over 40 years ago, and my life has never been the same. Once I understood that I could still deeply love Jesus, yet be in the business world, my life blossomed with opportunities. If I had become a pastor, I would have been very average and frustrated. Yet, as a business leader, my platform has allowed me to share Christ with my co-workers, customers, vendors, and competitors. I have been able to encourage marketplace leaders across the U.S. and around the globe. I shudder to think what would have happened to me had I not had that Saturday morning conversation in 1965. It was a defining moment in my life when I realized that I had been "called by God", but that calling was to be in the distribution business in the workplace as a full-time representative and ambassador for the King of Kings.

Let me say a few things about calling, position, and wrong thinking. As I stated in the introduction, dualism has infected our minds. We unconsciously believe that there is a sacred / secular divide. Being a minister for Christ is NOT an activity, a profession, a position, a title, a "higher" or a "special" calling, and does not require lengthy and expensive training. It is NOT a segment of our life, but an integration of all that we are. It is not as much what we do, as it is who we are. It is NOT what we are supposed to do to earn God's approval, but what we do as a response to His mercy and grace.

Being a missionary is NOT more pleasing to God than being a school teacher. It is the why we do what we do, and who we are becoming, as a missionary or a school teacher, that is important. Being a pastor is NOT more spiritual than running a business. My being a speaker is NOT more important than the work of a mother that is home today taking care of a sick child. Responding to God's call on our lives is more about <u>obedience</u> than some privileged separate class, more about passion than just duty, and more about our unique background, talents, personality, and gifting that He designed for us, than it is about any job description.

God has uniquely created you and chosen you to be His representative in a particular sphere of influence during this season of your life. He has all power and knowledge, and He will sovereignly engineer circumstances in your life. Yet, He will not violate your free will in providing you an arena for your calling to represent Him. He allows you to choose the best, or just the good, or even the bad.

There are countless stories in the Bible where God chose a specific woman or man for a task or an assignment. In 1 Kings 11:34 we read, *"for the sake of David my servant, whom I chose."* "But," you may say," David was special." Yes, but each of us is special to God. Each of us has a specific call upon our life. Once you understand that, you will view your workplace differently. Once you understand that God has <u>called you</u> to represent Him in your workplace and in every part of your day, your life will never be the same. In the next chapter we will find out <u>what</u> God wants us to do in our workplace.

Note: We will not take any more time to develop the subject of calling in this book, because many others have done an excellent job on the subject. If you would like to do more reading on this subject, I recommend *"The Calling"* by Os Guinness.

An Example from the life of Daniel:

Daniel was called to represent God in a pagan land.

"Then the king ordered...to bring in some of the Israelites from the royal family and the nobility...to teach them the language and literature of the Babylonians."

Daniel 1:3-5

Daniel was chosen by God as a young man of 14 to 17 years of age to be taken from his family in Judah by Nebuchadnezzar, King of Babylon, who had besieged Jerusalem. Daniel, along with three of his young friends, was forced into the king's service in this foreign land. Each of the Hebrew young men was assigned a Babylonian name. To Daniel, they assigned the name Belteshazzar; to Hananiah, Shadrach; to Mishael, Meshach; and to Azariah, Abednego. Just imagine your teenage son or daughter or your grandchild being taken to a foreign nation to be used there in the service of the king. God chose Daniel to be His personal ambassador to this powerful king, and Daniel had a tremendous influence on Nebuchadnezzar. You have been chosen by God to have such an influence on your superiors, co-workers, clients, associates, and competitors in your workplace. Only the living Christ can give you the spiritual power to do this impossible task. If He did it for a teenage Daniel in a foreign land, then He can do it for you today!

CHAPTER TWO
What are we to do?

OUR MISSION IS TO LOVE GOD AND LOVE PEOPLE

"Jesus replied: 'Love the Lord your God with all your heart and with all your soul and with all your mind. This is the first and greatest commandment. And the second is like it: Love your neighbor as yourself. All the Law and the Prophets hang on these two commandments'"

Matthew 22:37-40

As I sat in the lobby of the Hilton hotel with my vice president and one of my key field managers, I had to make a quick decision. Was I willing to pay the $30,000 that it would take for me to keep my word in honoring the third point of the Statement of Values that I had just presented to our entire sales force? God had forced me into a corner. Was I willing to pay real money for the words that were written on the piece of paper that I had just handed out to my 150 co-workers from across the country?

The story started nearly six months before when our distribution firm was chosen to be in a "family values survey" done by *Focus on the Family*, measuring how well our company modeled family values. During their final discussion with us, the Focus on the Family representatives noted that we had very strong values, but that they were not written down in a public form. They suggested that we should write out our values in a document which would be available for our employees and anyone doing business with us. So, we went through the process and came up with ten values based on the Ten Commandments. (See appendix three). We were very proud of them, and I had presented them to our outside sales and service team at our meeting. Now, fifteen minutes later God was asking me to take out my wallet and see how much I was willing to pay to honor them. My manager had tears in his eyes as he explained that he was traveling 70% of the time and was away from his family too much. We had determined years before that we would not do that, but we had lost business in his area and had to travel him out to keep him busy. Value #3 stated that the family was more important than the profitability of the company. If I moved him to another city, paid to sell his house, his travel expenses, and for his salary in the new city until we got enough business there, the total would cost us $30,000 or more. We agreed to do it.

One year later I got a two-sentence card from his wife. She said, "Thank you for moving us to Houston, Texas. You will never know what a difference it has made in our family." I thought that was great and a good ending to the story. I even shared it as I spoke to other Christian business owners across the country. However, a couple of years later I understood the rest of the story. As I was thinking about it one day, the Spirit of God seemed to mentally nudge me. You really did not get it, did you?" I admitted that I did not understand His meaning. The Spirit reminded me that the next year our business had grown 40%, and that most of that came in one city. You guessed it! The city was Houston, Texas. God will always protect you and reward you for obeying and honoring His principles. I am not implying that God's reward will necessarily take the shape of business success, but I do know that He "is a rewarder of those who diligently seek Him". (Hebrews 11:6) Our heavenly Father has a long-term vision as He shapes our character for His purposes through the circumstances in our workplace.

In chapter one, the key word was <u>calling</u>. It is a calling to represent Him. Now the key word is <u>focus</u>. We are to focus on our relationship with Him, so that we can love others with the love that we receive from Him. It really is fairly simple. We tend to complicate ministry with all of our seminars, books, conferences, and media. Jesus continually reminds us that it is all about <u>loving God and loving people.</u> He told us that ALL of the commandments are summed up in those simple words. When the focus of our heart is on God alone, then we will see each person from God's point of view, not as an interruption in our workday, but as a divine appointment and opportunity to show God's love. We do this by being sensitive, listening, and becoming available to each one that we encounter. Love is spelled T-I-M-E, and we have to learn how to do that as we go about our workday. I will examine that more in the next chapter.

The secret of how we get the power to love others is in becoming like Christ, who had the greatest capacity for loving even the most unlovely people. Paul wrote to the Galatians that he would persevere with them, even to the point of pain, *"until Christ is formed in you"*. (Galatians 4:19) As we spend time focusing on Christ, understanding His Word, and talking to Him in prayer, then we gradually become like Him. Mark 1:35 shows us that God's son, Jesus, made time with His father a priority, *"Very early in the morning, while it was still dark, Jesus got up, left the house and went off to a solitary place, where he prayed."* I have made it a habit to meet with God every morning for the last fifty years of my life. I try to include a devotional book such as Oswald Chambers' *My Utmost for His Highest* and a paraphrase Bible such as *The Message* or *The Living Bible.* I have also used the *One-Year Bible* for several years. It has kept me in the race when temptations and adversity tried to take me out. Psalms 5:3 promises that God will hear our petitions, *"In the morning, O LORD, you hear my voice; in the morning I lay my requests before you and wait in expectation."* I enjoy walking in the morning and just praying to the Father as I walk or ride my exercise bike. Paul tells us in Philippians 3:10 that the key of all of this is to really know Him and His power in our lives, *"I want to <u>know Christ</u> and the power of his resurrection and the fellowship of sharing in his sufferings, becoming like him in his death."*

As we fall in love more and more with our Heavenly Father and with His son Jesus Christ and His Holy Spirit within us, we prepare the soil of our hearts to be used by Him. People will be as receptive to us as we are receptive to God. Are we willing to allow the rocky soil of our independent hearts to be plowed up and transformed by Him? Are we willing to spend the time each day to be changed ever so slowly into the person that He can use in the lives of all of those hurting people around us in the workplace?

I must admit to you that one of my greatest faults is that for so many years of my life I have tried to DO things for Christ instead of falling in love with Him and let the overflow of that experience flow out of my life to others. My assistant of seventeen years once shared with me, "Kent, in the early years you were not mean or angry; you just viewed me as a machine. Work in and work out! You did not see me as a woman, a mother, a wife, and a real person." Gradually over the years as Christ began to form me into His image, I began to view her and my other co-workers not as machines, or company assets, or even as religious projects, but as people that God had placed under my care as a C.E.O. to love, care for, and protect.

When we are at our best for Him, we will not even think about it or realize that we are having an impact on those around us. We will simply manifest Jesus Christ to those around us through our thoughts, responses, words, and actions. As we are squeezed by the circumstances of the daily challenges of the workplace, the Holy Spirit will literally overflow out of us onto the lives around us. Jesus says in John 7:38-39, *"Whoever believes in me, as the Scripture has said, streams of living water will flow from within him."*

Oswald Chambers, in speaking about this overflow from our heart or our innermost being, explains it like this, *"Jesus said in effect, 'out of him shall escape everything he has received.' Our Lord always preaches anti-self – realization: He is not after developing a man at all, he is after making a man exactly like Himself, and the measure of the Son of God is self-expenditure. If we believe on Jesus Christ, it is not what we gain but what he pours through us that counts. It is not that God makes us beautifully rounded grapes, but that He squeezes the sweetness out of us. We cannot measure our lives by spiritual success, but only by what God pours through us, and we cannot measure that at all."* Chambers expounds on this when he says, *"Unless my life is the exact expression of the life of Jesus Christ, I am an abortion, an illegitimate. Experience must be worked out into expression; the expression is a strong family likeness to Jesus, and its mark is found in the secular life, not in the sequestered life."* [1] Oh, how I wish that we understood that today.

Paul reminds us in 2 Corinthians 3:2-3, *"You yourselves are our letter, written on our hearts, known and read by everybody. You show that you are a letter from Christ, the result of our ministry, written not with ink but with the Spirit of the living God, not on tablets of stone but on tablets of human hearts."* Chambers contrasts our expounding on God's Word verses living out the truth when he says, *"Christ in You...I may be an expert in a great many things...and I may be enchanted with the truth, but unless my enchantment is transformed into the energy, which bears the mark of the disposition of Jesus, it is making for spiritual inefficiency."* [2]

As we love the people around us out of the overflow of our relationship with Christ, we plant the seed of His love. Are we willing to die to our dreams, desires, plans, pleasures, power, possessions, and purposes? Are we willing to lay down our lives for others as He challenged us to do? In John 13:34, 35 (The Message), Jesus told the disciples, "Let me give you a new command: Love one another. In the same way I loved you, you love one another. This is how everyone will recognize that you are my disciples-when they see the love you have for each other." A secular survey stated that the workers in the marketplace have three needs: Dignity, Community, and Purpose. We can meet those needs by loving them, serving them, and sharing with them the true purpose of living.

---

[1] *The Place of Help*, Oswald Chambers. Grand Rapids: Discovery House Publications, 1989. pg. 140.

[2] *The Place of Help*, Oswald Chambers. Grand Rapids: Discovery House Publications, 1989. pg. 179.

As we love people it must be both <u>intentional</u> and <u>spontaneous</u>. God creates all of these opportunities, and we simply have to give the time and availability to respond to them. For example, I have intentionally worked at having a relationship with Frank, who is another C.E.O. in my monthly group. I have taken him to lunch and discussed his health issues and business problems and built a relationship with him. I purposely went by Linda's desk and asked how her mother was doing in the hospital. I spontaneously responded to the call at home from a co-worker who was put in jail and needed help and from a former co-worker who was being taken to the delivery room for her first child. Her boyfriend and the father had died a few months before of a heart attack. I needed to be there with her and her family. I have needed patience for long phone calls from key co-workers who lived in another city and needed attention and some personal care. We must remember as we minister as His ambassadors in the workplace that every person wants and needs to be loved. Our objective is to live out and communicate Christ's love to those around us. Loving God is all about our relationship to Christ, and we have to make it a priority. Loving people is also about time, and we have to put others before our own wants and needs.

One day my wife, Davidene, got a hand-written card signed by four of our female employees thanking her for being there for each of them. Each of them had met with her for a lunch, over the phone, or at our home for counseling. She did not even know that they had discussed these visits with their co-workers. One of the ladies has been helped in her marriage, one with an abusive situation, another was a new believer who we had led to Christ, and the final one was investigating the claims of Christ on her life. In most cases, you will never know the impact that you are having this side of eternity. And it is probably better that we do not know or we could become prideful. Jesus shows us just enough of the changes in others so that we will be encouraged to keep investing our lives into the lives of others.

So now we clearly understand that God has specifically called us to focus on loving God and loving people. In the next chapter we will carefully examine the place in which God wants us to impact those lives.

Note: If you would like to read further about this topic, Davidene and I have written the book *Show and then Tell, Presenting the Gospel in Daily Encounters* by Moody Press. It has over one hundred stories from seventy ordinary people. It will give you many ideas for loving people in your sphere of influence.

An Example from the life of Daniel:

Daniel continued to love God and love and respect his superiors while in captivity.

"But Daniel resolved not to defile himself...he asked permission ...'Please test your servants'...At the end of the ten days they looked healthier and better nourished than any of the young men who ate the royal food... To these four young men God gave knowledge and understanding of all kinds of literature and learning."
Daniel 1:8-17

Daniel chose to obey God and yet respect his superiors while in Babylon. He is a great example of how we can stand by our principles and yet honor those in authority over us. Daniel gave creative alternatives to his superior. We must always do exactly what our managers ask us to do unless it violates the values that we get from the Scriptures. But it is not always black and white. Sometimes we need others to help us see what we should do. That is why we need to be involved regularly in a small accountability group. Jesus modeled this principle with the twelve. Everyone who seeks to go into the workplace needs this regular interaction.

We also need an inner circle of three people who care about our soul and can be advisors and encouragers to us in the dark and difficult times. The three friends of Daniel are our example along with Peter, James, and John, the inner circle of Jesus. The three do not have to be in the same city, but you need to be able to interact with them by phone, or email, or in person. Take the time you need to find the three that will be your advisors for this season of your life. They may change as you go through the decades. You will not survive without these spiritual support systems in your life.

CHAPTER THREE
Where are we to do it?

OUR VISION IS TO START WITH THE PEOPLE AROUND US

"These commandments that I give you today are to be upon your hearts. Impress them on your children. Talk about them when you sit at home and <u>when you walk</u> along the road, when you lie down and when you get up."

Deuteronomy 6:6-8

I left work early one evening to go home for a sandwich and then to go on to our church. Several of us were planning to knock on the doors of newcomers in our neighborhood, tell people about Jesus, and invite them to visit our church. As I was driving, the Spirit of God seemed to ask my spirit a question. It was not an audible voice, but God clearly asked me, "Kent, where are you going?" I answered Him. Then He appeared to speak to my spirit and say, "It is great that you left work early because you are a workaholic, but why did you not just turn to the fellow at the next desk?" That executive had a thirteen-year-old child, who was on drugs. Why was I going across town to talk to someone that I did not know while my co-worker was facing a crisis? That question haunted me, and that night my life was changed forever. That was over twenty years ago, and for the last twenty years, my primary field of ministry has been my family first and my workplace second. If I have any time left over, I will work through my church or Christian organization.

Your workplace is very important to God. In the New Testament, 122 of Jesus' 132 public appearances were in the marketplace. Forty-five of the fifty-two parables of Jesus had a workplace context. Jesus spent most of his adult life in the workplace from the time he was a teenager until thirty years of age. He had only three years of public ministry. Most of the people in His home town knew him as a carpenter, not as a teacher. All twelve of the disciples came from the workplace, not from religious positions. Jesus did not want us to retreat from society or from the world, but He wanted us to engage it. In His famous prayer to the Father for us in John 17:15-18, Jesus prays, *"My prayer is not that you take them out of the world but that you protect them from the evil one. They are not of the world, even as I am not of it. Sanctify them by the truth; your word is truth."* So, God wants us to represent Him in our workplaces to those who do not know Him. Most of them will not seek out our churches, but everyday they are at the next desk to us in the marketplace.

You are probably familiar with verses 4 and 5 in Deuteronomy 6, where we are commanded to love the Lord with all of our heart, soul, and strength. However, in the next verses, printed above, we are commanded to do this as we sit around the table with our family, as we get up in the morning, and as we go to bed at night. Then we are told to do it as "we walk along the way". That is the secret to representing Christ in our workplace. It is not a religious activity. In fact, I do not encourage people to take their church or religion to their workplaces; they just need to take the Christ that lives within them. We do not have to have a prayer meeting, read the Bible, have a religious service, or grab people by the collar and ask about their eternal salvation. We simply let Jesus Christ flow out of our lives as we go through the workplace with all of its challenges, pressures, joys, and relationships. As we go, we simply keep focused on God, love the people around us, and meet their needs. (We will discuss how to do that in the next chapter.) As I speak to groups on this subject, I start walking back and forth across the room. They finally get it! Ministry in the workplace is NOT an activity but a way of life. This takes the pressure off of you.

The problem is that we have carefully divided our lives into the segments of our job, home, extended family, health, finances, church, social life, and then evangelism and discipleship. God wants us to live an integrated life where ministry encompasses all of the activities of our daily life. He intends for us to spiritually impact the lives around in each of those areas. The result is that there is no division between the secular and the sacred. Look at the charts on the next page. In the top diagram, "ministry" is an activity. In the bottom diagram, "ministry" encompasses all of life.

— Frustration/Segmentation —

— Focused/Integrated —

Acts 1:8 tells us, *"But you will receive power when the Holy Spirit comes on you; and you will be my witnesses in Jerusalem, and in all Judea and Samaria, and to the ends of the earth."* This clearly gives us the different places that we are to go as ambassadors for Jesus Christ and lists them in order from our closest priorities to the most far reaching ones. Let me make this analogy:

- Jerusalem - My family, close friends, and my co-workers

- Judea - My customers, suppliers, and associates in my distribution business

- Samaria - My competitors and people that I meet in passing

- World – Those in Asia, Europe, Africa, Latin America, and the rest of the world

Henry Blackaby has spoken a number of times at our Fellowship of Companies for Christ International Conferences for Christian business owners who want to use their businesses as a platform for serving Christ. Henry has often said, *"Watch and see where God is working and join him there…understanding what God is about to do where you are is more important than telling God what you want to do for Him."* So many of us want to go to another part of our city, or across our nation, or to another country to do some important mission work for Him. However, the most important place to have a long-term influence for Christ is with the person that we interact with everyday in our workplace.

When Jesus healed the hurting people, they often wanted to go with Him. But, in most cases he commanded them to <u>return</u> to their homes, workplaces, and cities. Yes, He did call the disciples to leave their comfortable surroundings and follow Him. But that was the exception, not the rule. Jesus told the demoniac to "return home" (Luke 8:39), the blind man gave testimony to the religious leaders that he had received his sight (John 9:25), the paralytic was told to take his mat and go home (Matthew 9:7), and the woman at the well ran back to the men of the city to tell them what Jesus had said (John 4:28). You are the most valuable to

Jesus Christ right in your ordinary sphere of influence. That is where you are investing the majority of the hours of your life, in your family, with your close friends, and in your workplace. The longer the time that we have in any one workplace location, the larger the influence that we will have with those around us. I was at the same desk for nineteen years and the same firm for twenty-eight years. Over those years I was able to have a large influence with my co-workers, vendors, customers, and business associates that is still yielding dividends today.

One day I was flying back from Chicago on a business trip. I had gone up to meet with one of our largest vendors. The company was a leader in the black hair care industry in which we were one of the largest distributors in the nation. During the visit I had met with the leadership of the firm and each of the four children of the founder who were now running the manufacturing company. They put me up at a nice downtown hotel, they paid for my airline ticket, and they entertained me with some wonderful meals. I had a super time during my 48-hour visit as we discussed new products and where the industry was going. As I flew back home, a thought came to me. I had not paid for all of these costs. My firm had not even paid for them. My church or Christian organization had not paid a dime for me to go on the trip. My supplier had paid the total cost. My time was my only contribution. Yet, I had represented Christ in my workplace. I had modeled and spoken for Him.

This same type of thing occurs every day in the workplace as the secular marketplace takes followers of Jesus into homes and offices and stores and factories across our land. The employers and companies pay for the cars, trains, trucks, and airplanes to transport people across the city, the state, the nation, and the globe to represent their companies and to represent the risen Christ. In fact IBM and Coca Cola will pay employees to move overseas from the U. S. to Asia or Europe or the Middle East and give them a wonderful salary to represent them in a foreign nation. They meet and relate to ordinary folks as they live there, but they also associate with powerful government and business leaders. (I have often wondered why we do not let these multinational firms pay for part of our mission budget.) These believers are assimilated far faster into the nation's network of influencers than are normal missionaries. This is really BAM or "Business as Mission", a concept which is changing the face of missions.

Our family sold our general merchandise distribution firm about ten years ago. I stayed on for three years as the CEO. By that time we had about 400 employees scattered out in 40 cities over 30 states. Once or twice a year we brought our 160 people from the field into Oklahoma City or Dallas or Houston for training and encouragement. These meetings were always very busy for me but were a great time of interaction, fun, and strategic discussions with our key leaders. A couple of years after we had sold the firm (but I was still CEO), I was to address the participants on the last day of the weekend meeting on a Sunday morning. The Saturday night before this meeting, I was alone in my hotel room finishing the preparation for that Sunday morning address. As I was preparing, the Spirit of God seemed to speak to me. God wanted me to throw my notes into the trash. I was a little discouraged because I had worked on my talk for a couple of weeks. However, I tried to listen to what God was asking me to do. I asked Him, "What do you want me to say to them?" He seemed to say, "Kent, just tell them that I love them, and that the reason that you stayed on for this time as the CEO, is that you love them also."

So, on that Sunday morning, following a voluntary chapel service at which half of the attendees chose to worship, I stood up before my co-workers from around the nation to deliver my little talk. I had worked with some of these folks for twenty-eight years, and this would be my last address to these people who were so important to me. I told the men and women, some of whom I had worked with for many years, that the reason that I had stayed on for these years after selling the firm was to help them and the new owners. My motivation was that I loved them and that I wanted to be involved in their lives as we together served major retailers across our nation. I affirmed them that, although business was getting very tough and consolidating, our firm had an excellent service reputation. We were a survivor in a tough industry. I went on to tell them that God loved each of them.

Then, I shared with them the story of the man at the next desk that I shared with you at the beginning of this chapter. During the story, I did not notice it, but one of our ladies ran out the back door of the theater in which we were meeting. We were at a large conference hotel right next to the Houston Intercontinental Airport. So, when I finished my talk and got to the back of the room, I was told that "Sheri" was in the women's rest room, that she was crying uncontrollably, and that she wanted to talk with me. So, I agreed to meet her in a large empty conference room across the hall, next to the ball room where our people would be eating in a few minutes. As we sat down, Sheri was sobbing. I tried to ask her what the problem was, but she continued to cry. I asked, "What did I do to offend you? What did I say?" All that Sheri could say was, "My son, my son!" Finally she blurted out, "My 13-year-old son is at home, and he is on drugs. And I do not know what to do about it!"

Well, I was totally unprepared for that. I so wished that my wife, Davidene, was here at the meeting and could handle this situation. Like most men, I am not very good at handling an emotional crying woman. In most cases, if I do meet with a female employee, I try to have another woman sit in on the conversation or have the woman talk to my wife or a trusted Christian co-worker, who can counsel when needed. In this case, the meeting was wrapping up, so I met with Sheri alone. I did not have my Bible, but I could quote the verses I had memorized. I explained to Sheri that we could not help her son today, but that we used a chaplain service and they would contact a local pastor in her city in Ohio who would help with her son's situation. I could, however, help her.

So, I asked her permission to share with her how she could have peace in the midst of this terrible situation. She gave me permission through her tears. Over the next few minutes I shared with Sheri the simple Gospel, drawing illustrations and listing Scriptures on a blank piece of paper. I then asked Sheri if she would want to ask Jesus Christ into her heart. She surprised me with a huge "YES"! I led Sheri in a short simple prayer. That is the last time that I have seen Sheri.

About three months later, we lost the contract with a large drug chain in the Midwest part of the nation, which was Sheri's major account. So, Sheri left our firm and went to another job. About six months later, when Davidene and I were writing our first book, we contacted Sheri and asked if we could tell her story in the book. We asked how she and her family were doing. Sheri said that her family was active in a local church and that her son was doing much better. Our families still exchange Christmas cards. The point is that I had little idea that Sunday morning that Sheri had a son on drugs, or that she would respond to my story, or that I would never see her again. We just have to be available to God to be His personal representative in our corner of the marketplace. There are hundreds of Sheri's and Bill's in your sphere of influence to whom God wants you to model His love.

I have been able to do this with a number of my co-workers over the years, and I have found it advantageous to have a few counseling tools in my office. The best, of course, is a modern version of the Bible. I also like to have a few evangelistic tracts, such as "Steps to Peace With God" from the Billy Graham Association, or "The Four Spiritual Laws" from Campus Crusade.

NOTE: We used a workplace chaplain service for 17 years in our distribution firm. The chaplains did an outstanding job of serving our employees in times of crises, death, marriage problems, financial issues, sickness, etc. I believe that the number one method of evangelism to adults in the U.S. is corporate chaplaincy. I think that every pastor and church staff worker should serve as a paid or volunteer chaplain at least one day a week in the workplace. It would totally change how we do church and equip our people to represent Christ in their workplaces. Today our manufacturing firm uses a chaplain service for our plant. We find it to be the most important benefit that we can give to our people. These chaplains do not take away the responsibility of the business owner or the Christian co-worker. It takes all three, the owner, the fellow employees, and the chaplain working together to represent Jesus to the large percentage of workers who will never attend our churches on Sunday.

You will find some chaplain ministries listed in Appendix II; Workplace Organizations.

An Example from the life of Daniel:

Daniel represented God and spoke for Him in the toughest of workplaces.

"When the commander...had gone out to put to death the wise men of Babylon, Daniel spoke to him with <u>wisdom and tact.</u>'Why did the king issue such a harsh decree?' Arioch then explained the matter to Daniel. At this, Daniel went in to the king and <u>asked for time,</u> so that he might interpret the dream for him...Then Daniel returned to his house...to his friends...He urged them <u>to plead for mercy</u> from the God of heaven." **Daniel 2:14-18**

In your workplace today you may be facing the possible loss of a client or your job or even your business. You probably are not facing the loss of your life as Daniel was. He and his three friends were part of the group of "wise men" who were advisors to the king. Because the king became frustrated with the lack of help from the entire group, Daniel and his friends were in danger of being put to death with the group. So Daniel prayed and asked God for divine wisdom in order to help the king and save their lives. He also asked his friends, his "small group", to pray with him.

So many times we think that we have the worst workplace environment. We believe that no one has it as bad as we do. I would suggest for you to go to the inner city or travel to any of the nations around the world where I have been. Get your eyes off your situation and focus them on God. He will provide for you in the specific workplace that He has assigned to you. Just as Daniel prayed, you can pray daily and ask for His provision for the challenges of the day. Review the character of God and praise Him daily for His sovereignty, power, presence, knowledge, grace, mercy, love, eternal nature, truth, immutability, justice, righteousness, and holiness. When we, like Daniel, get our eyes off our surroundings and circumstances and onto His plan for us, then we gain the vision to see our circumstances from His point of view. That changes everything.

CHAPTER FOUR
How are we to do it?

OUR MINISTRY IS TO SERVE, LOOKING FOR OPEN DOORS

"Not so with you. Instead, whoever wants to become great among you must be your servant, and whoever wants to be first must be your slave— just as the Son of Man did not come to be served, but to serve, and to give his life as a ransom for many."

Matthew 20:26-28

My vice president and I walked slowly to our car in the parking lot of the headquarters of the largest retailer in our nation. We had just lost a ten million dollar account. That was a third of our thirty million dollar nationwide distribution business. We both knew that many firms could not survive losing that much business at one time. When we had arrived for our appointment, just two hours earlier, we had really thought that we could save all of the business, or at least part of it. We had faithfully and honestly served this retailer for seven years. They had a corporate policy to buy direct, and not through distributors, but they needed our expertise on this category, African American hair care products. The percentage of these customers could vary from 3% to 90%, so the flexibility of a distributor was beneficial to their stores. But, finally, the corporate pressure from the top to eliminate the distributor was just too great. They treated us with integrity and gave us a 60-day notice.

We would have to drive back the four hours from Arkansas to Oklahoma City. We knew that we would have to make immediate cuts of at least 25% of our people and that many others would take pay cuts. I turned to my VP and told him that we needed to pray and thank God that we lost the business. He looked at me like I was a crazy man. I asked him, "Is God no longer all powerful? Is He no longer sovereign? Did this move catch Him by surprise? Does He no longer love us and care about our people?" He finally agreed, and we bowed right there in our car in the parking lot and thanked God that we had lost a $10 million account. We just trusted God that He had something better for us.

Many times through the years we would experience the loss of 10% to 15% of our business for various reasons, such as companies going out of business, or a changing of management policy to go direct and eliminate distributors. However, we grew our business most years through good service, new categories, new customers, and acquisitions. We acquired twenty-three firms in twenty-three years and expanded while in a declining industry. However, this was the biggest challenge that we would face.

Within eighteen months we made back every bit of the business through gaining some new customers and a key acquisition of another competitor. We were grateful to God, and it was just one more trial of our faith that was rewarded as we clung to His promise that He would provide for us and our people. He did this time after time and is still doing it today in our manufacturing business in the most difficult economy of my lifetime. But, as in many of my other stories from the marketplace, that prayer in the parking lot was not the end of the story.

Fifteen years later we were in the medical distribution business and only had a few employees. Our young VP was in Arkansas looking for a broker for a new line of products that we were trying to put together. He interviewed Dennis for the position. Dennis asked him about the principals of the distribution firm. Our VP, Clay, explained that Kent Humphreys was one of the principals. When Clay mentioned my name to

Dennis, Dennis immediately said that he would take the job. Clay asked if he wanted more information. Dennis shared with Clay the rest of the story. Dennis explained that he was the purchasing agent who had kicked our firm out of the large retailer some fifteen years before. Within just 90 days, he realized that it was the worst decision of his twenty-five year buying career. He reported to his supervisor that it was actually costing the retailer more money to buy "direct from the manufacturer" than it was to go through us as a distributor. Dennis asked if he could reverse the decision, but he was overruled by the policy from the top. So, Dennis told Clay that we had served them with integrity and excellence for those seven years and that he would gladly represent our small medical firm if we so desired. Wow! You never know the impact and the results of your service to your customers or your relationships in the workplace over the years. People are watching your actions, and very seldom do you know the results of your testimony for Christ.

How do we represent Christ in a secular workplace? How do we love people where God has placed us? It is really fairly simple. We just <u>serve</u> them! By dying to self, we express Christ's love to others by making eternal investments into their lives. We do this by our attitudes, our words, and our actions in concert with other believers as we <u>serve</u> together using our various gifts. Our number one problem is patience, but by being both intentional and spontaneous, we can be caring, encouraging, and loving as we allow the Holy Spirit to work through us, even under the most difficult of circumstances. <u>Then after establishing trust, we simply walk through the open doors of opportunity.</u>

I shared with you an example of serving a customer, so let me give you a similar one concerning a vendor. This will again show you the importance of long-term perspective and patience. In 2004, I was speaking to the Korean International CBMC convention of Christian business leaders in Seattle, Washington. Out of 400 attendees, I was one of only two people who did not speak Korean. I was to speak on Friday evening and arrived at the last minute for the opening dinner on Thursday night. As I was finishing my meal, a man named Henry came to my table and introduced himself. He asked if I remembered him, and I could not. He asked if I remembered his firm, Sunny Marketing, and I immediately remembered that we had purchased import products from them in the late 70's and early 80's. We talked for awhile and then Henry shared with me his story. He shared that by watching me and two other business leaders for fifteen years, he finally decided to come to Christ. He saw me send Christmas letters sharing the Gospel in a non-religious way every year. He silently watched me pay my bills on time and treat my suppliers with integrity. Every day he was listening to our words and seeing how we conducted our business.

I had NO idea that I ever had any influence on him, and his firm was a minor vendor for us. So, Henry told me that the next evening before I spoke, he had asked permission of the conference director to introduce me. He spoke for a few minutes in Korean. I do not know what he said, but I knew that I would have the attention of the audience. Henry's testimony was worth far more to the audience than anything I could say. Do you realize that your actions today can have an impact on your co-workers and associates ten, or twenty, or thirty years later? That is what I call a long-term investment!

People will never know that we love them if we do not <u>show it by serving them</u>. Jesus reminded us that serving others is the key to showing God's love. People cannot know our hearts if they do not see our actions in the mundane circumstances of life. Saint Francis is often quoted as saying, "Preach Jesus, and only if necessary, use words." We are not to take religion to the workplace, but we are simply to bring the aroma of Jesus Christ to those around us.

Let me give you a very practical example. A few years ago I was attending our FCCI Conference of Christian business owners. The speaker suggested that if we wanted to make an impact on our co-workers, we should give up our parking place. Well, the Holy Spirit convicted me to do just that when I returned home. It was really hard; after all, I had earned the place right next to the door. I enjoyed driving right up to the door instead of looking for a place among several hundred spaces. But, I finally got up my courage and parked on the back row one icy morning. I got out of the car and slipped on the black ice. Now I knew how all the other people felt, and I sheepishly thought that God had a good reason to look down from Heaven and laugh at me. I permanently gave up my space for a new program. Each month the employees elected a co-worker who showed the best servant heart. That person got to use my old parking place for the next month. Everyone loved it but me, because I continued to park at the back of the lot. This humbled me and allowed me to show my co-workers that I cared for them.

OPEN DOORS

I am now going to share with you perhaps the most important part of this book. I want to show to you the simple steps that you need to go through in order to serve others and show them the love of Christ through practical actions. The Scriptures show us very plainly exactly what steps need to take place. If you have your Bible, please turn to Colossians 4. Let us see what God has for us in this key passage.

COLOSSIANS 4:2-6 NASU

- "Devote yourselves to prayer…"

- "That God will open up to us a door for the word, so that we may speak forth the mystery of Christ"

- "Conduct yourselves with wisdom toward outsiders, making the most of the opportunity…"

- "So that you will know how you should respond to each person"

Paul gives us the first step in verse two: pray. That is a hard thing to do, particularly for strong leaders who want to DO something for God. Without prayer, most of our efforts will just turn into proud fleshly deeds with little results. In verse three, he says that God will open the door. We do not have to kick it down. For many years I thought that I had to make something happen in relationships or force the conversation to spiritual things. Only in the last few years have I tried not to do as much or be so busy, but to look around and see in which lives around me the Spirit of God is working. This is a much better plan and is far less frustrating.

Then, Paul says in verse five that we are provided with an opportunity beyond the open door. When we walk through the door, we see the opportunity that God has already provided for us, and we do not have to manufacture a situation or force the timing. Verse six explains that we simply must respond to the opportunity that God has provided inside of the open door. Wow! Is that simple or not? I know that you just cannot believe that it is that simple. In the past few months, I have tested this time and time again. I just wait by my phone and email and have casual meetings in the workplace. I am able to minister to people that I have never met through divine appointments. I am able to encourage and help business leaders literally around the globe because I am learning this principal of praying, watching for the open door, seizing the opportunity, and responding at the moment of God's prompting. Let's examine some practical ways of implementing these principles.

PRAYER

1. Make a list of twelve people in your workplace, neighborhood, or school.

2. Begin to pray for them by name on a regular basis.

3. Ask God to make you sensitive to them and to use you as He is working in their lives.

You may need to make a list like the one on the next page. We have provided a blank form and one filled out with examples. Then, you simply build relationships over the days, weeks, months, years, and maybe even decades with these family members, friends, and co-workers. You just continue to pray for them, love them, serve them, and be their friend.

I used three categories to divide the twelve people who I placed on my chart, and I suggest that it would be helpful for you to do, as well. The first category is those people whom we know are believers or "followers of Jesus". For those people, we are looking for opportunities just to serve them. We may be involved in encouraging or exhorting or even discipling them. We just want to be used by the Holy Spirit to help them move farther down the God's pathway in their walk of becoming closer to Christ.

The second category is comprised of the people whom we think or discern have <u>not</u> yet trusted Christ. In this case we are looking for the opportunity to model Christ to them and have an opportunity to share the Gospel with them, once we see the open door (we will explain this next).

The third group consists of those whom we are unsure where they stand with Christ. With these friends we will simply share the Gospel when we have the opportunity. If they have already trusted Christ, they probably are not walking close to Him, or we might be able to see it in their lives. So, for this person, we may be either trying to lead them to Christ or helping them in their walk with Christ, which may be in the baby stage, somewhat dormant, or fairly immature at this time.

WORKPLACE PASTOR
Co-worker/Contacts

	Need	Resource	Action/Date
Believers			
John	Insensitive Husband	Marriage Seminar	Give Scholarship to Seminar
Joe	Eager-growing Christian	Mature Friends	Invite to Small Group
Nancy	Young Children	CD/DVD	Loan DVD on Raising Kids
Linda	New Christian	One-Year Bible	Give for Birthday
Non-Believers			
Bill	Teen on drugs	Youth Leader-Skill	Introduce at Lunch
Jane	Marriage Difficulty	Chaplain Program	Offer his services
Ann	Death of Father	Cards/Booklets	Mail over 12 months
Larry	Financial problems	Small Group-Finances	Give him phone number of leader
Un-Sure			
Don	Wife lost job	Business Contacts	Write letter of recommendation
Joan	In hospital-surgery	My Attention/Time	Visit at Hospital
Mary	Poor self image	Tool Chest	Send Birthday Card/Book
Herb	Unknown	Christmas Letter	Add to Christmas List

WORKPLACE PASTOR
Co-worker/Contacts

Need	Resource	Action/Date
Believers		
Non-Believers		
Un-Sure		

Seven Key Crises

One day a crisis will occur in the life of someone with whom you have a relationship. All of us have crises from time to time. In fact, one or several of those co-workers working closely around you will probably have a crisis the next few months. These crises can come from many sources, but here is a list of some common areas:

1. Birth of a new baby
2. Death of a loved one
3. Major illness
4. Marriage problems
5. Children issues
6. Financial difficulties
7. Major Loss - of job, home, position, etc.
8. "Baby Boomers" dealing with aging parents

Ten Steps in Ministering to Others

We have built relationships based on love, we have prayed, and then the crisis occurs in the life of our co-worker. We can now follow the ten steps below. We are careful to listen first and not be quick with easy or "canned" or "textbook" solutions. We continue to earn that person's trust by serving, caring for, and encouraging them. We finally earn their trust to share the gospel with them, disciple them, or become a counselor or mentor to them.

1. **OBSERVE** the crisis.
2. **MEET** immediate needs.
3. Be **SENSITIVE**.
4. **LISTEN**, even when it is inconvenient at times.
5. Be **AVAILABLE**.
6. **SERVE**.

7. **CARE** for them.

8. **ENCOURAGE** them.

9. **LOVE** by actions and attitudes.

10. Verbally **COMMUNICATE** God's love.

Let me give you an example of how this would play out as I relate to a co-worker named Joe.

1. I have been *praying* for Joe for months.

2. I hear that Joe's mother has died (crisis).

3. I know that he is going through the normal grieving process (observation).

4. I send Joe a card with a personal note and continue to pray (sensitivity).

5. I listen to Joe over a coffee break about what he is doing to settle her affairs (listen).

6. I ask Joe to go to a basketball game with me during the next few weeks. I also miss a much needed lunch break to listen to him again (availability).

7. I offer to help Joe go to pick up some furniture from his mom's home that he is selling (servitude).

8. I send him a booklet of Scripture (caring).

9. I drop him a note to let him know that I am still praying for him months later (encouragement).

10. I get a call from Joe late one night about his teenager who is in trouble. I listen, trying to encourage and counsel him. I am there for him (show love).

11. Finally, I ask Joe if we can read the Scriptures together. Eventually, I ask if he would like to invite Jesus into his life.

Remember, this is a Kingdom focused ministry primarily done in the workplace. It is not a "church activity" or a religious obligation. It is based on relationships. We have to be intentional about what we do. We have to build bridges with Joe through our workplace connection *before* the crisis occurs in his life. We are extending the walls of the church out into our natural sphere of influence.

Sharing the Gospel

Let me say a few words about sharing the Gospel and what happens after your friend prays to receive Christ. In the USA today we are no longer a "Christian nation" with most people having a religious or church background. We are now secular, and many of our friends and co-workers have no religious or church background at all. This change has occurred over the last two generations. So, the method I used to share the Gospel when I was in college forty years ago (Campus Crusade's *Four Spiritual Laws*) and my favorite one to use in many other places fifteen or twenty years ago (Billy Graham's *Steps to Peace with God*), are much more difficult for people to understand today. I still use the Navigators' *The Bridge to Life* many times when I am sharing with a person who is totally open and ready to trust Christ. This is also useful for sharing the Gospel with a person that I meet for a brief time and may never see again. However, most of those that we build long term relationships with will not be won to Christ in one event or one setting. We must build bridges, answer their questions, and be willing to invest months or years in patiently bringing them to Christ. (See Appendix I for these three evangelism resources and related web sites.)

Follow-up with Discipleship

This book is not so much about <u>what</u> we share in the "evangelism" process as much as it is about <u>how</u> we build bridges of relationships and look for open doors in order to have the opportunity to share. There are hundreds of great books and courses on "How to Share Your Faith", and I will not seek to duplicate their efforts. Neither is this a book on "discipleship". The Navigators and others have given us tremendous resources in the area of discipleship. As I shared in chapter one, I was an intense follower of Jesus at an early age. By divine appointments, God brought a number of godly men into my life as a teenager and in my twenties to help me in my walk with Christ. I was discipled with a group of other young leaders in my twenties by a business leader who invested much into my life.

As we looked at Colossians 1:28, 29 in the introduction, I stated that there are two things that we are commanded to do. First, we are to naturally share Christ (evangelism) and secondly, we are to teach others (discipleship). When God allows us the privilege and joy of leading someone to Christ, we then have a responsibility as a spiritual parent to help them get on the right pathway. The decision to trust Christ is just the beginning, the birth of a new life with Christ. So, we must make sure that we do not leave the baby there in diapers without any milk and tender loving protective care. We need to help them in several key areas:

1. Give them a Bible and show them how to read a few verses each day. Ask them to start in the Gospel of John and perhaps you can discuss what they are reading with them. Use a Living Bible or Message Bible or one that they can easily understand. (God's Word is God speaking to them.)

2. Show them how to PRAY in short easy sentences. (They are learning to talk to God and listen for His voice.)

3. Get them into a small group of other believers in their neighborhood, office, or church.

4. Point them to a Bible believing church near their home. It could be your church, or one that is closer to their religious background if they have one.

5. Finally, arrange to personally meet with them on a regular basis for a few weeks or months, or you can turn them over to someone else who knows how to disciple a newborn Christian. During these times together, you can get them started in the

basics of their new life in Christ. The tools mentioned in Appendix I will be a great help to you in this process.

In many cases, I have led someone to Christ on an airplane, or a co-worker who lived in another city, or an employee who was several management levels below me in the workplace, and it was impractical for us to meet regularly. So, I had to follow them up by phone or e-mail, or I had to find another person to whom I could "turn over" this new baby in Christ. In any case, we need to not drop the handoff. Satan would love for us to think that this is not important and miss this critical step. CBMC has an excellent resource, *Operation Timothy*, that has helped many in the workplace in basic follow-up and discipleship. Corporate Chaplains has designed an excellent resource called *The Compass*. The Navigators have a wealth of materials to help, as do Campus Crusade and many other workplace ministries. See Appendix I for these tools and the related web sites.

THINK STRATEGICALLY, FROM A SERVANT'S PERSPECTIVE

1. How can you serve a family with a new baby?

2. How can you care for a co-worker or a neighbor facing surgery?

3. What can you do with a friend who is facing marital difficulties?

4. What about someone who is having financial problems?

5. How can you show your concern when a friend mentions having discipline problems with a child?

6. How would you help a parent who has a teen with a drinking or drug problem?

7. How would you handle a co-worker who has a spouse that has lost their job?

You Can Take Christ to Your Workplace

1. Do NOT take religion to work – take Christ!

2. Lift up the flag, but do not be offensive.

3. Be a light in a world of darkness.

4. Offer to pray for co-workers with problems.

5. Actually write down the problem, pray about it, and check on them later.

6. Ask about their families.

7. Keep a supply of Bibles and booklets to give out in the right situation.

8. A hand-written card is a sign of caring.

9. Say 'thank you'!

10. Go out to lunch and talk as you travel together.

11. Always <u>pray</u> first, preparing your heart and theirs.

12. Look for where God is at work in the lives of others; watch for that <u>open door.</u>

13. Be <u>patient</u> – this is a process, not an event.

14. As you walk through that open door, identify which <u>opportunity</u> you need to address first.

15. <u>Respond</u> carefully and with sensitivity; this person is NOT a project but a relationship that God has brought into your life for His purposes.

16. They want to know that you <u>care</u> for them before they will listen to what you have to say to them.

17. They will look for examples of your <u>character</u> and integrity. They want to know if it really works in your life before they will buy into what you "preach" to others.

18. It is "<u>caught</u>", not "taught", and they will watch you closely. This takes TIME!

19. This type of evangelism and discipleship takes places in our sphere of influence and is NOT about activities, but about <u>relationships.</u>

20. Pray…Pray…Pray

21. Read the Gospels, and look at the example of Jesus Christ loving and serving people.

EXAMPLES OF SOME ACTIVITIES THAT HAVE WORKED IN A BUSINESS ENVIRONMENT

Here are a few examples of what we did in our distribution firm over a twenty-year period. Every year we learned something new. It is exciting to be creative. Not everything works, but people will know that you care. Just do not be too religious, and you will not burn any bridges.

1. Give away books, especially children's Bible story books, books on parenting teenagers, and finances.

2. Give out The Message Bible.

3. Give out the foreign language Bibles for ethnic employees.

4. Give away the One-Year Bible at the year's end.

5. Give cards to those who are sick, make hospital visits, and make up Grief Kits (for 12 months of care).

6. Send birthday cards – signed, with personal notes.

7. Write a monthly letter to employees and spouses, "My Heart to

Yours". Put it in the pay envelope.

8. Send a Christmas letter to all employees, customers, and vendors.

9. Send appropriate holiday cards to Jewish competitors.

10. Send employees' children to Christian summer camps.

11. Send helpful biblical tools to customers and vendors, like "The Message Proverbs".

12. Have Christmas company dinners.

13. Have summer picnics for the entire family.

14. Send willing employees and their spouses on marriage retreats.

15. Say THANK YOU in person, by card, by phone, by email, by awards of every kind.

16. Give a pizza lunch for new employees every week for six weeks with the CEO or business owner. Use the time to discuss the company's values.

17. Give monthly cookouts in the summer.

18. Offer company chaplains.

19. Celebrate Mother's Day for the entire week. Give a small token of appreciation every day. (a card, a flower, candy, e-mail note, etc.)

20. Give a Christmas gift to employees and their families. We tried several ideas, but the best received was a basket with a movie ("It's a Wonderful Life"), popcorn, and a note to "Take your family to the movies".

I could share with you hundreds of stories, but we do not have the space for all of them in this short book. Many of them are available to you in our other books and on our audio CDs. However, let me expound on a few of the suggestions above. Every year we sent out thousands of copies of a Christmas letter to our employees, customers, vendors, and competitors. We would share the Christmas story in a non-religious way using current events or a captivating story. We sent the book of Proverbs from *The Message* to our vendors. We told them it was the best business book ever written, and we noted 25 business principles and the page numbers. I remember that one corporate buyer returned it saying that he could not receive "gifts". Yet, the next week a CEO sent me a personal note thanking me for the valuable book. So, you never know the response that you will have. We sent our employees' kids to a Christian non-denominational summer camp. The parents were amazed and thankful when their children came back totally changed. The best thing that you can do for your people is to help their kids. We gave away children's Bible story books to the mothers and grandmothers that worked with us. We gave away books on marriage and raising teenagers and finances. During times of grief, we sent something to the person every month for the next twelve months. The list of creative things that you can do is very long, and I learn new ways to impact our people all the time.

I know that all of these suggestions may be a bit overwhelming. Remember that we learned all of this by trial and error over thirty years. So, take your time. Do what fits your circumstances and your workplace environment. You may say that you are not a business owner or CEO or manager. That is OK. Most of the effective actions have to do with relationships and spending time with other people. If you are in leadership, then you can affect the overall culture, but you actually have less opportunities with individuals. If you are not in leadership, then you have more of an opportunity to have close relationships with your co-workers and workplace associates. Be creative and come up with your own ways of showing God's love and serving others. The Holy Spirit is very creative and will give you marvelous ideas if you are listening and attentive. In the next chapter, we will see when we need to start these relationships.

An Example from the life of Daniel:

Daniel served as an advisor to four
different kings in difficult circumstances.

*"There is a man in your kingdom who has the spirit of the holy
gods in him. ...he was found to have insight and intelligence and
wisdom like that of the gods. ..your father ...appointed him chief
of the magicians, enchanters, astrologers and diviners. This man
Daniel...was found to have a keen mind and knowledge and
understanding, and also the ability to interpret dreams, explain
riddles and solve difficult problems. Call for Daniel, and he will
tell you what the writing means."* **Daniel 5:11-12**

Daniel was a servant. He served King Nebuchadnezzar and
King Belshazzar of Babylon, King Darius the Mede, and
finally Cyrus the Persian. Each of these came to trust Daniel
because he served them with honesty and wisdom and gave
them the truth of God. Daniel earned the right to be able to
share spiritual insights and wisdom from God, as a coach to
each of these kings. He did not "tell" them what to think or
do, but, by using discernment and carefully worded questions,
he coached each king through the process, while giving God
the credit for his wisdom. His enemies carefully watched him
and could find no fault in him.

Even with his excellent track record, he eventually faced death
because one of the kings was tricked by the enemies of Daniel.
Daniel had to daily trust God that he would be able to survive
in this difficult work environment in a foreign land. Daniel
was not self-righteous or religious or pushy about his faith. He
simply lived out his relationship with God in a pagan
workplace. He is a model to all of us today.

CHAPTER FIVE
When are we to do it?

OUR MANDATE IS TO SEE THE LOST REDEEMED BY CHRIST, STARTING NOW!

"When He looked out over the crowds, His heart broke. So confused and aimless they were, like sheep with no shepherd. 'What a huge harvest!' He said to His disciples. 'How few workers! On your knees and pray for harvest hands!'" Matthew 9:36-38 (The Message)

"Well, I am telling you to open your eyes and take a good look at what's right in front of you…It is harvest time!" John 4:35 (The Message)

I opened the envelope from "Tammy" and began to read the five-page hand-written letter. I had worked with Tammy in our distribution firm some four years earlier. I had seen her once since that time. She shared with me the pain of her life over the last few months. She had been abused by her husband, lost her job, lost her health, and was financially and emotionally a broken person. She asked for an appointment with me. I took the letter home and had Davidene read it carefully and give me some advice. Davidene said that I needed to meet with Tammy and that it appeared she desperately needed Jesus in her life. I asked my assistant and Tammy to come in and see me, and since she knew Tammy, I wanted her to sit in on the visit.

Tammy came and began to tell her sad story for about 30 minutes. We both listened carefully. It was just amazing to me that when she was at the end of her rope, Tammy sought out a former employer that she had not known well. I had had few dealings with her because she had worked in our warehouse, and I normally worked with the office and field staff. It was obvious that Tammy wanted emotional help and was not seeing me just to get financial advice. She was genuinely interested in what I had to say.

After some time, I gently asked Tammy if I could share some Scriptures with her that would give her hope. Over the next few minutes, I simply shared with her how much God loved her and how she could come to know Christ. About 30 minutes later, Tammy prayed to receive Christ. We were able to give her a Bible, some helpful pamphlets, and some financial advice. We gave her a lot of Scriptures on hope. I sent some encouragement cards to her every few days for several weeks. She spent a lot of time in God's Word over the next few weeks. She began to attend a local church. She got a new job and got back on her feet financially. God had brought a person from my workplace, who was just an acquaintance a few years before, into my life for a brief time just so that I could help her go to the next step in her spiritual journey. Then she went on with her life. This is what I call a divine appointment. God wants to give us many of them, but we are usually too busy in our jobs or families or religious activities to see the hurting people around us.

Changed lives! That is the bottom line. As laborers, we get to reap the harvest that God has already prepared. We take hurting people out of darkness and despair into life, light, and fulfillment!

Bruce was one of my very closest friends for some 35 years. We had met Bruce and his wife, Linda, as young couples when Davidene and I had returned to Oklahoma City after four years in the military. Our older daughters had been born on the same day and our younger daughters were born just a few weeks apart. Our families took vacations together, and we went to the same church for a number of years. Bruce was one of my "Inner Circle" for over thirty years. We were in a small weekly men's group together for probably twenty of those years. For about seventeen years, we were in the apartment real estate business as partners. So, Bruce and I knew each other in various contexts and were the closest of friends.

Then one morning I got a call while I was traveling and speaking in India. Our team of Christian business leaders from FCCI was on a five-city tour doing seminars to help establish small groups of Christian business leaders in each of the five cities. We were leaving our hotel on a Sunday when I got the call. Davidene shared that Bruce had died suddenly of a heart attack the day before while attending a business conference. I was shocked. Bruce was 59 years of age and appeared to be in excellent health. I was the last person in Oklahoma City to see him alive because his plane for the east coast had left within minutes of ours going to India. He had given me a big smile and hug as we boarded our plane. We had met by "accident" at the airport that morning. God had allowed me to see my best friend one more time.

It took me about 24 hours to make arrangements to leave our team and fly back to the United States for the funeral services. I got back with a day to spare, and the family asked me to be one of the three men who spoke at Bruce's memorial service. I remembered that Bruce and I had had lunch just a week earlier. We had concluded the lunch with both of us encouraging the other to "finish well" in our walk with God. I was a little jealous of Bruce because he had passed the test and done that. Now he was with Jesus in eternity. At the end of the service, after the three of us and the pastor had spoken and the music was completed, we offered to those in the large audience an opportunity to say a few brief words.

Over the next few minutes many work associates and friends came to the microphone. One by one a number of the men said that Bruce regularly met them for breakfast or lunch. They stated that Bruce was the closest friend that they had. Bruce was always there for them. I knew that Bruce had made me feel important and cared for by visits, emails, and voice messages when I would travel. I felt his prayers and encouragement. I know that he met with other guys. However, I had NO idea that he had

12 to 15 people who considered him to be their "closest" friend. Some of these were from Kansas, Florida, and Washington D.C. Wow! What an impact Bruce had on so many lives. He had certainly finished the race well!

Bruce was an ordinary guy just like you and me. He was not any more talented or gifted than you are. He struggled to balance work and family and church and relationships just as each of us do. He worked long hours at times, but he still had time for his wife, Linda, and his daughters and his grandchildren and his many close friends. Bruce and Linda were also a part of our seven couple "Empty Nesters" group of friends. Bruce had the same temptations and doubts and trials that all of us face, but he steadfastly pursued his walk with Jesus Christ. He continued to follow the calling of God on his life as a business leader by loving the people around him and serving them. He was at the hospital, at the home of those grieving, and celebrating life by having fun at the lake or snow skiing or traveling to the beach with his family. Just as I had, Bruce had sensed a call to vocational ministry as a young man and was a youth minister for a number of years. Yet, Bruce found himself in the workplace and learned how to minister to his co-workers for over thirty years. Bruce modeled the message of these pages, and YOU can do the same.

When I was a young business leader, I wish that I had known the lessons that I have learned over the last thirty years. I was so religious and tried so hard, but I had few results. I tried to make things happen and do things for Jesus. My heart was right, but most of my methods were wrong. I tried to force results instead of looking where God was at work in the lives of the people around me. Today I take a very different approach. I simply try to practice the principles that I have shared with you from the Scriptures and follow the leading of the Holy Spirit. As a businessman, I make investments in small companies, real estate, and in oil. As a follower of Jesus, I make investments in people.

I have the privilege of speaking to a lot of university students each year. From those groups I invite the students to come and have lunch with me and discuss the workplace. A few of them take me up on it each year. Some of those relationships have extended for many years. I first met my business partner, Brian, as a student; then we met once every year or so for many years. This developed into a mentoring relationship and eventually we became partners in a small distribution business. Many of the young men that I meet call me, and we have lunch every year or so to share what is going on in our lives. These occasional mentoring relationships are a real joy to me and an encouragement to them. I hope that you are investing your life into those around you through discipling, mentoring, coaching, modeling, and just casual relationships. It is really ALL about RELATIONSHIPS. Jesus modeled that with the three, the twelve, the men and women close to Him, and the seventy that He sent out two by two. The harvest is plentiful, but the laborers are FEW. God wants you to be available to invest into the lives that you come into contact with everyday.

FRUIT TREES

Let me close our time by sharing with you a story from my good friend, Jim. I have shared this story around the world because it is so applicable to what we are trying to say in this concluding chapter. Jim lived in Oklahoma City a number of years ago. He was in a men's Bible study with Bruce and me. Jim was in the technology industry and was one of the sharpest business guys that I have ever met. He also had a heart for other men and investing into their lives. One Saturday Jim decided to plant some fruit trees in his back yard. In Oklahoma City, we have few trees. The city is surrounded mainly by flat wheat fields. So, Jim went to the nursery and asked about buying some fruit trees to plant in his back yard. He asked how long it would take for the fruit trees to bear fruit. The man replied that it would take only four to five years. My impatient friend, Jim, thought that was too long, and he went home without the trees.

About five years later, Jim was sitting on his patio in his back yard. He was not able to pick any fruit, because he had no trees. He had not taken the time to plant a few trees five years earlier. Now he realized how foolish he had been. All he would have had to do was to bring home a few small trees, plant them, water them, and put on some fertilizer from time to time. It would have taken very little effort or money. If he had just done that, then he would be picking fruit today! We may want to laugh at his stupidity, yet, we do the same thing. We look at others in our church or sphere of influence, and we marvel at how God is using them. We wonder how they have such ministry in the lives of other people. Yet, we do not see that those are simply the results of seeds that they had planted in their own life and the lives of others years before. We have been spoiled by our instant microwave age! We expect immediate results and are not patient or willing to make long-term investments into the lives around us.

SEVEN LAWS OF THE HARVEST[3]

Jim's fruit tree story is a vivid reminder to us about the laws of the harvest. John W. Lawrence in his classic book, *The Seven Laws of the Harvest: Understanding the Realities of Sowing and Reaping*, lists the seven laws that never change. Jesus reminds us that it is harvest time, so we followers of Jesus need to understand the irrefutable laws of the harvest. Those Seven Laws are:

1. We Reap Only What Has Been Sown

2. We Reap Only the Same Kind That Was Sown

3. We Reap in a Different Season Than We Have Sown

4. We Reap More Than We Have Sown

5. We Reap in Proportion to What We Have Sown

6. We Reap the Full Harvest of the Good Only if We Persevere; The Evil Comes to Harvest on Its Own

7. We Can Do Nothing About Last Year's Harvest, Only This Year'

Therefore, just as the seed must die in the ground to produce a crop, we

---

3   *The Seven Laws of the Harvest: Understanding the Realities of Sowing and Reaping.* By John W. Lawrence. Grand Rapids: Kregel Publications, 1995. pg.130.

as followers of Jesus must "die to self" and give our lives to love and serve people in our sphere of environment. We must patiently plant seeds into the lives of those around us. We may labor in our workplaces for long periods of time without seeing immediate results. We may labor for ten or twenty or even thirty years until we see the fruit in the lives of some of our co-workers or friends. Yet, God is in charge of the harvest. He knows when the fruit will be ripe. At that time, He will allow us to reap the harvest in the lives of those hurting people around us. He is the master of the harvest and knows all things. Our only responsibility is to build relationships, love people, serve people, and be ready at any time to reap the harvest that He will prepare.

An Example from the life of Daniel:

Daniel could not change his habits after 69 years in captivity

"Now when Daniel learned that the decree had been published, he went home to his upstairs room where the windows opened toward Jerusalem. Three times a day he got down on his knees and prayed, giving thanks to his God, just as he had done before."

Daniel 6:10-11

So, have you figured out how old Daniel was when they threw him into the lions' den? Was he over 20 years of age? The majority of people think that Daniel was a teenager, or at least under 30, because that is what the pictures show in most of the Sunday school literature. Or was he over 40 years or age or even 50 years of age? The fact is that in Daniel 6, when he was put into the lions' den, Daniel was 82 or 83 years of age. He had been in captivity for nearly 70 years.

Since he had the habit of praying three times a day, he continued doing so, even at the risk of his life. I probably would have negotiated with God and just quietly prayed in my closet. I might have reasoned with myself that I was more useful to God alive than dead, because I was one of the three vice presidents and was up for the number two slot right under the king. But, Daniel put it all on the line and continued to open his windows toward Jerusalem and pray three times a day. He was put into the lions' den and God spared his life for future service. What a story of the faithfulness of Daniel for all of those years.

...continued

Daniel understood his calling even in a foreign land. He loved God and served the rules of a pagan empire. He lived out his calling as God's ambassador in the most secular of workplaces. He patiently honored God as an advisor and leader for the entire captivity of Israel during the 70 years in Babylon, which was later invaded by the Medes and then the Persians. Daniel stands as our example of how you can live out the integrated spiritual life walking with God in the most secular of environments. Daniel showed us how to walk through open doors and impact the culture in which God sovereignly places us.

CONCLUSION

As we proclaim Christ naturally in our families, communities, and workplaces, we need to understand five simple truths:

1. We have been called to represent Jesus Christ as ambassadors for Him in our workplaces.

2. Our mission there is to love God and love those whom God has placed around us.

3. Our vision must be to start with those closest to us everyday in the workplace.

4. Our ministry is to simply serve them, looking for Open Doors into their lives.

5. Our mandate is to see the harvest of lost ones redeemed by Christ, starting right now.

Let me close by sharing with you a couple of verses that have been very encouraging to me. *"God looks down from heaven on the sons of men to see if there are any who understand, any who seek God."* Psalms 53:2. The Psalmist tells us that God is looking for those of us who are seeking Him. He longs for us to seek Him and be active for Him in His harvest field. And He will strengthen us and give us all the help that we need if we are fully committed to Him. *"For the eyes of the LORD range throughout the earth to strengthen those whose hearts are fully committed to him."* 2 Chronicles 16:9. May each of us daily see Christ at Work opening doors in our workplaces which will allow us to impact others for His glory!

APPENDIX I
Resources for Evangelism and Discipleship

Maestro Worklife Coaching
A Self-Directed web-based coaching system by Doug Spada
www.worklife.org

The Compass
A tool to help new followers of Christ by Lanphier Press
www.lanphierpress.com

Operation Timothy
Discipleship tool by CBMC
www.cbmc.com

Discipleship studies and tools
Navigators and NavPress
www.navpress.com

Steps to Peace with
God by Billy Graham
www.billygraham

The Bridge to Life
www.navigators.org

The Four Spiritual Laws by
Campus Crusade
www.campuscrusade.com

APPENDIX II

Recommended Workplace Ministries / Web Sites

Lifestyle Impact Ministries
Kent and Davidene Humphreys

www.lifestyleimpact.com

Fellowship of Companies for Christ Int.

FCCI / Christ@Work

www.fcci.org

Blackaby Ministries

www.blackaby.org/marketplace

Business as Mission Network

www.businessasmissionnetwork.com

Business by the Bible
Crown Financial Ministries
www.crown.org

Business Proverbs

www.businessproverbs.com

C -12 Group**

www.C12group.com

CBMC (USA)

www.cbmc.com

Christianity 9 to 5 (Professor Michael Zigarelli)
www.epiphanyresources.com

Christians in Commerce
www.christiansincommerce.org

Convene (formerly BBL Forum) **
www.convenenow.com

Corporate Chaplains of America
www.chaplain.org

Crossroads Career Network
www.crossroadscareer.org

Executive Ministries
www.execmin.org

Faith and Work Resources
www.faithandworkresources.com

Full Gospel Business Men's Fellowship
www.fgbmfi.org

Inside Work
www.insidework.net

Integrity Resource Center
www.integritymoments.com

International Coalition of Workplace Ministries

www.icwm.net

International Christian Chamber of Commerce

www.iccc.net

Intervarsity-Urbana-Whole Life Stewardship

www.urbana.org/whole-life-stewardship

Lausanne Business as Mission

www.lausanne.org

Marketplace Chaplains USA

www.mchapusa.com

Marketplace Leaders

www.marketplaceleaders.org

Marketplace Network

www.marketplace-network.net

MEDA

www.meda.org

Priority Associates (Campus Crusade)

www.priorityassociates.org

Releasing Kings

www.releasing-kings.com

Scruples (YWAM)
www.scruples.net

Selling Among Wolves Sales Seminar
www.sellingamongwolves.net

Strategic Christian Services
www.gostrategic.org

Wise Counsel**
www.askwisecounsel.com

Worklife
formerly His Church at Work
www.worklife.org

Avodah Institute
www.avodahinstitute.com

**These organizations primarily serve CEO's and business owners through small groups that meet weekly or monthly.*

APPENDIX III
STATEMENT OF VALUES

Our values are standards by which basic business choices and decisions are made. They are revealed in the context of personal relationships (example: Buyer to Supplier, Service Person to Store Manager, Manager to Employee, etc.). The integrity of a firm's structure is dependent upon its values. These values should be evidenced by our behavior to each other and to those outside our firm. The sum of all of our behavior, which reveals our values, represents our "corporate culture". We do not possess our values as a company in order to succeed; rather, we believe we will succeed because of our values.

The following values represent the substance of our firm's foundation. They exemplify our spirit, the very essence of that which we consider worthwhile, important, and significant. We will treasure and prize these values by our words, thoughts, actions, and even our motives. We will build our company on what they represent.

1. TRUSTWORTHY WITH INTEGRITY

We will be reliable, dependable, and can be counted on to keep promises. "We will do what we say we will do" within the promised time frame.

2. WORTH OF THE INDIVIDUAL

We will practice the "Golden Rule" in decision-making. We will respect human life, dignity, and rights of each including the consideration of their health, safety and work environment. We will seek to give positive affirmation and recognition. We are in business for "people" (employees, customers, vendors), not for our own wealth, power, prestige, or ego.

3. FAMILY AND STABILITY IN RELATIONSHIPS

The family is the foundation unit of every society. We will respect women as wives, men as husband, and singles. The family has a higher priority than the firm and its profitability; therefore, we will seek to build it up, not tear it down.

4. HONEST AND TRUTHFUL COMMUNICATION

We will strive to be genuine, open, and aboveboard in all relationships. We will honestly and accurately report the facts.

5. RESPONSIBILITY OF THE INDIVIDUALS AS A PART OF A TEAM

For the use of our time, talents, and company resources. Each of us will accept individual accountability for how we carry out our responsibilities. We, as a company, will aim to motivate each other by praise rather than criticism so as to create an atmosphere of productivity and freedom to admit individual mistakes in order to accomplish our team goals.

6. BALANCE OF WORK/REST

Vacations and breaks will be encouraged so that proper rest, recreation, and reflection will maximize the long-term effectiveness and productivity of the individual and the entire team. We believe in working hard, but not necessarily in working unproductive long hours just for the sake of appearance.

7. REWARDING PRODUCTIVITY

In every way possible (example: praise, monetary, promotion, awards, benefits, etc.), we will seek to reward industriousness, innovation, initiative, prudence, and discipline. Our focus is to develop our full potential, the natural results of which is reaping the rewards of our labor.

8. EVERYONE IS ACCOUNTABLE TO AUTHORITY

Any enterprise must have structure and organization. Every person is accountable to a higher authority.

9. SERVANT LEADERS

Within every organization there are many managers, but few leaders. Effective leaders will be servants who have attracted a following because of their passion, vision, integrity, and love for their people. We will make every effort to develop this kind of leader.

10. STEWARDSHIP

We will strive to use wisely and prudently the resources with which we have been entrusted.

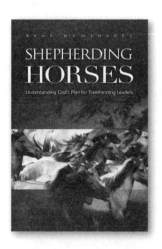

Shepherding Horses (Volume I)
Understanding God's Plan for Transforming Leaders
(Lifestyle Impact Publishing)

Kent's most well-received book yet! This 50-page guide to Understanding God's Plan for Transforming Leaders is a must-read for any pastor and the strong and driven business leaders (horses) that he shepherds. Kent looks at a biblical view of "horses" and shares with pastors an effective way to partner with these business leaders – building bridges of acceptance and understanding.

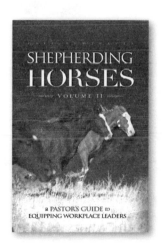

Shepherding Horses (Volume II)
A Pastor's Guide for Equipping Workplace Leaders
(Lifestyle Impact Publishing)

In this book, Kent encourages pastors to invest in the incredible resource they have – the business leaders in their churches. The book is full of practical and possible ideas for shepherding, encouraging and releasing these leaders for ministry in the place they understand best - their business world.

Housekeeping Skills for Kids
Teaching Them Doesn't Have to Be a Chore
(Lifestyle Impact Publishing)

Davidene's book, Housekeeping Skills for Kids: Teaching Them Doesn't Have to be a Chore" has proven to be a best-seller. In it she provides simple and practical steps for parents of any-aged children to train them in skills that they will need to create and run their own home someday. Full of stories, encouragement, and ideas, this book is an inspiration to any parent trying to develop their kids' domestic skills. It covers everything from cooking, to organization, to use of tools, to planning great parties.

Encouragement for Your Journey Alone
Meditations of Hope for Widows
(Tate Publishing)

This wonderful little book is a gift of hope and encouragement for widows. It is a compilation of meditations, which the author suggests reading at the pace of one per week. This gives thinking and praying time over each meditation. Kent Humphreys has written a letter each month for nine years to many widows; this book has been birthed from that long-standing ministry and is a special gift to women who have a special place in God's heart.

Between the Phone Call and the Funeral
(Tate Publishing)

Have you ever wondered what to do for a grieving family? Do you find yourself taking food to the house, feeling a bit nervous about what to say? Do you end your visit by saying something like, "If you need anything, call me"? You mean it, but you are not sure what would be helpful. This book is your answer. It is the best gift you could give, and the ideas in it are the best things you could do for these hurting friends. Buy one now, and have it before you need it, because you will need it. Buy another one to put in your church's office for the next church family who needs it. Helping those who grieve is a wonderful ministry, one which blesses the giver as much as the receiver.

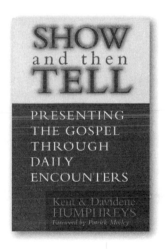

Show and then Tell
Presenting the Gospel Through Daily Encounters

(Moody Publishing)

How can we become confident in sharing our faith, both in action and word? How do we make ourselves available to others, Christian and non-Christian, to share what God has done in our own lives? How do we encourage them to trust God more? In Show and then Tell, Kent and Davidene encourage Christians that God has called every one of us to evangelism. He has given us unique personalities and gifts to reach our world for Christ. Our lives have extraordinary possibilities when we call on Jesus to give us the strength to share our faith – naturally.

Christ@Work – In Your Transition

From the Campus to the Workplace

(Lifestyle Impact Publishing)

College grads and graduate students will find this to be a helpful resource as they transition to the marketplace. Campus ministry leaders from the major ministries, business leaders, pastors, and leaders on Christian college campuses help the graduate to navigate the change. Topics from getting a job, to finding a church, making a budget, and learning how to live a balanced integrated life in their new environment will provide a wealth of wisdom to the graduate. This valuable handbook will be useful to grads for years to come.

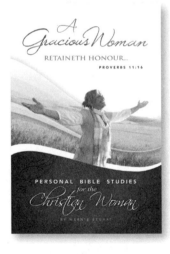

The Gracious Woman Retaineth Honor...

Personal Bible Studies for the Christian Woman

(Lifestyle Impact Publishing)

The Gracious Woman, which was originally written by Mernie Stuart, has been revised and re-published by Davidene Humphreys, Mernie's daughter. It is comprised of 24 lessons, including such subjects as "The Christian Woman and her relationship to God, to her husband, to her children, and to her community." A complete teacher's guide is available, so this is an ideal course of study for an individual or a group.

FIND THESE BOOKS AND MORE AT

Lifestyle Impact Ministries
PO Box 271054
Oklahoma City, OK 73137
405-949-0070 x101

www.lifestyleimpact.com

LIM is the resource ministry of Kent Humphreys and his wife, Davidene. Access our website for free downloads of ministry letters and handouts, PowerPoint presentations from various speaking engagements, audio recordings and more.